Dear Ms. Barber

Coming in 2016:

Dear Ms. Barber: Managing Children's Behavior, Volume II

Dear Ms. Barber

Managing Children's Behavior

Volume One

Brenda Fisher-Barber

Library and Archives Canada Cataloguing in Publication

Fisher-Barber, Brenda, 1963-, author
    Dear Ms. Barber / Brenda Fisher-Barber.

Contents: Volume one. Managing children's behavior.
Includes parenting advice columns by author originally
    published in the Penticton herald.
ISBN 978-0-9948638-0-5 (volume one : paperback).--
ISBN 978-0-9948638-2-9 (volume one : bound)

    1. Child rearing. 2. Parenting. I. Title.

HQ769.F58 2015   649'.1   C2015-905666-7

Acknowledgements

Thank you to all of the parents, children and families I have had the pleasure of working, playing, learning and singing with over the past thirty-five years, and to all of my amazing early childhood education (ECE) college students.

You have all helped me to understand and appreciate the gifts and treasures from the early years of childhood along with the wonderful, rewarding journey of parenthood.

*Parents aren't the people you come from.
They're the people you want to be, when you
grow up.*

~ Jodi Picoult

For my son,
Jeffrey Sydney Barber,
also known as Jeff, and affectionately as "Bubba":
My wish for you is that you may find love,
happiness, balance and success in all of your life's
experiences and that you never forget that you
have made my wonderful journey through
parenthood and life, as your mom, a very special,
exciting and tremendously fulfilling experience.

You are a gift that I treasure daily and always.
I love you to the moon and back again!
Thank you for teaching me as well.

A huge thank you to my mom and dad,
Art and Lanore Fisher,
for the most amazing childhood,
full of adventures and learning,
unconditional love and support and
positive models.
I am the parent I am today
and a positive model for others
because of you!

Childhood is that stage which ends the moment a puddle is first viewed as an obstacle instead of an opportunity.

~ Kathy Williams
www. thenaturalparent.co.nz

Dear Ms. Barber

From January 2011 through March 2013, the Penticton Herald carried "Dear Ms. Barber." This popular column was written by Brenda Fisher-Barber, an early learning expert with over thirty-two years' experience working with children of all ages. At the time, Brenda was a StrongStart coordinator with School District 67 at Queen's Park Elementary School, with eighteen years' experience instructing college students in early childhood education (ECE) courses. She also had experience as a foster parent and preschool teacher, and was raising a teenage son.

Dear Reader

This wonderful book you are about to read is the first for me and I am very excited to share twelve of my parenting advice columns I wrote in my hometown of Penticton for the Penticton Herald. I want to thank Andre Martin and James Miller for the rewarding and exciting opportunity they gave me. I thoroughly enjoyed answering parent's questions and offering ideas, support and strategies in my column.

Along with twelve of my favorite columns, I have also included new and current ideas and research on managing children's behavior, along with my own personal experiences as a parent and early childhood educator. I am excited to share strategies and tools, real life experiences and small discoveries for coping, nurturing, enjoying and surviving the early years with your children.

I hope that parents and caregivers will recognize aspects of themselves and their children in my columns within these chapters and remember that, unique though our own experiences may be, not one of us really travels this path alone.

Parenthood is truly what binds us together. Our own doubts and questions awaken empathy for parents everywhere and our fierce love for our own children deepens our compassion for all children. I encouraged parents and caregivers to write to me for over two years and I was honored to share advice and support with them so that somehow I was able to ease the way for them on their journey with their children through childhood.

~ Brenda Fisher-Barber, a.k.a. Ms. Barber

Contents

The difficulty of the journey sometimes turns out to be its blessing.
~ Marianne Williamson

Chapter One

Managing Children's Behavior and Parenting Styles

My philosophy of managing children's behavior has always come from a place of respectful, loving understanding and consistent interactions and communication. My style of parenting and care giving has always been within the "authoritative" style. The authoritative parent is warm, loving and caring while establishing rules and guidelines their children are expected to follow. My parents were wonderful models of this type of parent and I have raised my son with this style of management as well.

My son, college students, parents of children I have taught and anyone who has asked me for advice will tell you that I thoroughly enjoy re-searching and constantly educating myself on a variety of positive and effective ways to communicate with children and to manage their behaviors. When my son, Jeff, was younger, he used to say, "Mom, I wish you didn't do so much research and have so much learning." I would laugh and hug him, and now I reflect on how he must have felt having a mother who thought she had all of the information and answers on parenting. In all honesty, he taught me many lessons on how to navigate through parenthood with a positive outlook and attitude, with humor and the philosophy of "choosing my battles." Thank you again, Jeff.

This *Volume One* edition you are reading is full of healthy, positive and effective ideas that will attempt to answer some of those questions you may have on parenting, managing behavior and nurturing a healthy and happy child in a respectful and loving way.

During the 1960s, psychologist Diana Baumrind conducted a study on more than 100 preschool-age children (Baumrind 1967). Using naturalistic observation, parental interviews and other research methods within homes and childcare centers, she identified four important dimensions of parenting:

1. disciplinary strategies,

2. warmth and nurturance,

3. communication styles, and

4. expectations of maturity and control

Further research by Eleanor Maccoby and John A. Martin also suggested the addition of four parenting styles (1983):

1. authoritarian,

2. authoritative,

3. permissive, and

4. uninvolved.

Authoritarian parenting: In this style, children are expected to follow the strict rules established by the parents. Failure to follow such rules usually results in punishment. These parents fail to explain the reasoning behind these rules. They have high demands, but are not responsive to their children's emotional needs. According to Baumrind, these parents "are obedience-and status-oriented, and expect their orders to be obeyed without explanation" (1991).

Authoritative parenting: Like authoritarian parents, those with an authoritative style establish rules and guidelines that their children are expected to follow. However, this parenting style is much more evenly balanced.

They are responsive to their children and willing to listen to questions and concerns and offer explanations for their actions. When children fail to meet the expectations, these parents are more nurturing and forgiving rather than punishing.

Authoritative parents understand their children and love them unconditionally. They are teachers and mentors for their children.

Baumrind suggests that these parents "monitor and impart clear standards and rules for their children's conduct. They are assertive, but not intrusive and restrictive. Their disciplinary methods are supportive, rather than punitive. They want their children to be assertive as well as socially responsible, and self-regulated as well as cooperative" (1991).

Permissive parenting: Permissive parents, sometimes referred to as indulgent parents, have very few demands to make of their children. These parents rarely discipline their children because they have low expectations of maturity and self-control.

According to Baumrind, permissive parents are "more responsive than they are demanding. They are nontraditional and lenient, do not require mature behavior, allow children to behave in any way they choose and avoid confrontation with their children" (1991). Permissive parents are generally nurturing and communicative with their children, often taking on the status of a friend more than that of a parent.

Uninvolved parenting: This style is characterized by few demands, low responsiveness and little communication. While these parents fulfill the child's basic needs, they are generally detached from their child's life. In extreme cases, these parents may even reject or neglect the needs of their children.

After learning about the impact of parenting styles on child development, I wondered why all parents simply did not use an authoritative parenting style. After all, this parenting style is the most likely to produce happy, confident and capable children.

I have learned that some of the potential causes of these differences include culture, personality, family size, parental background, socioeconomic status, educational level, and religion.

Of course, the parenting styles of individual parents also combine to create a unique blend in each and every family. For example, the mother may display an authoritative style while the father favors a more permissive approach. In order to create a unified approach to parenting, it is essential that parents learn to cooperate and communicate effectively as they combine various elements of their unique parenting styles.

I have found from my own experiences, that the authoritative parenting style provides advantages over the other styles. Children of these parents are happier, more capable and successful in social competence and have higher self-esteem. They perceive their parents' requests as fair and reasonable and they are more likely to comply with the requests. These children understand the reasons for rules and boundaries and feel loved and nurtured instead of unloved and "bad" for their misbehavior.

Lastly, these children are more likely to internalize (or accept as their own) the reasons for behaving in a certain way and then they achieve greater self-control. I wrote a column on self-regulation and will explain this term further in Chapter Six.

Here's a column about parenting styles. This one focuses on an issue every parent faces sooner or later: the power struggle.

Dear Ms. Barber:

My husband and I are constantly battling with our three-year-old, who engages in power struggles with us on a daily basis.

He constantly tests our limits, refuses to get dressed and ready in the morning for pre-school and other scheduled outings, and has become very defiant with food and other requests.

Is this normal? My other friends have children that are so easily managed and compliant when we are out with them, and I am so concerned that this is not just a stage but part of his personality. Should we be worried? Is this normal?

~ Power Struggle Parents in Penticton

Dear Parents in Penticton:

Power struggles can be a common occurrence with most toddlers and preschoolers. They can also resurface now and again throughout your child's life.

Although they are difficult to deal with, you will be relieved to learn that young children who attempt to engage in power struggles are actually developing at an age-appropriate level. It is a typical and natural step in their growth and development and these children are learning that they have their own ideas, feelings, and strong desires and that these are different from those of the adults in their lives.

This type of behavior is an important intellectual leap, but with it arrives behavioral changes.

While their behavior may be extremely frustrating to you and your husband, keep in mind that children in this stage are constantly exploring their world in order to develop and learn new skills and understanding.

Testing your limits and boundaries is just another way that they explore their surroundings and make sense of rules and order.

Children need parents and adults to establish firm limits and boundaries that are consistent and expectations that are age-appropriate and to show them loving, caring and respectful management. Your children need to learn at a young age that the rules of adults exist for good reasons, that those rules must be followed and that the adults will continue to love and support them through this stage of growth and development.

When children are young, I have found that offering choices in the clothing they wear, foods they eat, etc. will help set up a more positive, empowering experience for all involved. For example, you are the one to set out two pairs of pants, shirts or shoes for your child to choose from and they will feel empowered when they get to choose instead of being told what to wear.

Empowered children are more easily managed and have a greater sense of accomplishment than those who are constantly told what to do and when to do it!

Also, give children a five- to ten-minute warning, if possible, for transitions and changes in schedule so that they are able to "switch gears" from what they are doing and prepare for the change. I have also used an egg timer, a five-minute sand hourglass, songs and games to help children move from one transition to the next, to allow for a positive learning environment.

Respectful management of children will help to develop positive responses and reactions in your children.

For more about dealing with power struggles, I encourage you to read the book *Positive Discipline*, by Jane Nelsen. As she points out in one of her chapters:

Power struggles create distance and hostility, instead of closeness and trust. Distance and hostility create resentment, resistance, rebellion (or compliance with lowered self-esteem).

Closeness and trust create a safe learning environment. You have a positive influence only in an atmosphere of closeness and trust where there is no fear of blame, shame or pain. Remember that it takes two to create a power struggle.

Adults need to remove themselves from the power struggle without winning or giving in and create a win/win environment by offering choices when appropriate.

Nelsen details eighteen steps and suggestions to limit and deal with power struggles (along with other behavioral issues), and I highly recommend her book to all parents.

Lastly, please remember that all children behave differently in the home with you than they do out in public with others. They share all of their emotions, negative and positive, with you, the ones that love them unconditionally.

Parenting is a challenge and we need to show up every day with our "bag of tools" and start fresh each day with a renewed outlook and a clean slate on guiding our children through every stage of their growth and development.

Good luck on your journey!

~ Ms. Barber

You have a positive influence only in an atmosphere of closeness and trust where there is no fear of blame, shame or pain. Remember that it takes two to create a power struggle.

~ *Jane Nelsen*
Positive Discipline

Children learn more from what you are
than what you teach.
~ W.E.B. DuBois

Chapter Two

Temper Tantrums

It's a familiar scene: You are standing in line at the grocery store with your preschooler, almost finished checking out. For the fifth time in a row, your child asks for a piece of candy that is strategically placed at children's eye-level in the checkout line. You have repeatedly said no, when suddenly, the tantrum and angry outburst begins. His legs and arms flail, and then he lets go with an ear-piercing scream, and begins hitting the floor. Meanwhile, between muffled apologies to those in line behind and frantic bagging of groceries, you attempt to get as far away from the store as possible.

Why do preschoolers have temper tantrums? We expect toddlers to have them when they're unable to communicate their wants and needs due to lack of language and emotional growth, but preschoolers should be past that, shouldn't they?

Actually, understanding why a preschooler has tantrums can be the first step in knowing how to deal with them. Preschoolers are toddlers with a year or more of life experiences and growth behind them, so it is not unusual for them to have tantrums for some of the same reasons. Some of those reasons include:

- being tired due to too much activity,

- being hungry while on the go,

- being angry or frustrated,

- not getting what they want, when they want it,

- feeling neglected and wanting attention, and

- wanting more independence, to be able to do things for themselves but not being able to yet.

I have learned over the years that how you handle temper tantrums plays a large part in how a preschooler will act when he or she is older. While having tantrums is a normal part of a child's development, how you choose to react and deal with them is entirely up to you. No matter how embarrassing your preschooler acts in public, don't give in to them. It is so important for them to learn that you are the guide and teacher and that you make the decisions. You will also want to be sure to tell them that you love them and you are telling them "no" for a very good reason.

It is much easier to prevent temper tantrums than it is to manage them once the volcano has erupted.

Here are a few tips I have learned over the years and have practiced for preventing tantrums and some things you can try:

- Reward children for positive attention rather than negative attention. During situations when they are prone to temper tantrums, catch them when they are showing positive behavior and say such things as, "I like how you are sharing your toys with your friend" or "Nice job sharing your toys with your friends."

- Give children control over little things whenever possible by giving them choices. A little bit of power given to the child who is seeking more independence can hold off the bigger power struggles later. "Which do you want to do first, brush your teeth or put on your pajamas?"

- Distract children by redirection to another activity or idea when they tantrum over something they should not do or cannot have. "Let's read your favorite book to-gether" or "We can have your special treat or snack at home as soon as we buy our groceries."

- Choose your battles. Teach children how to ask or make a request without a temper tantrum and then honor the request.

- Make sure that children are well rested and fed in situations in which a tantrum is a likely possibility. Say, "Dinner is almost ready. Here is a cracker or carrot for now."

- Increase your tolerance level. Are you available to meet the child's reasonable needs? Evaluate how many times you say "no." Avoid fighting over minor things.

- Keep a sense of humor to divert the child's attention and surprise the child out of the tantrum.

Try to do your best to stay calm and cool during this trying time. Let your children know that their needs are important and that you want to help them. Tell your children you understand they are frustrated, hungry, or tired. Ask them to calm down and to help you decide how to work it out. They need to know that you will listen and that you want to help them learn to deal with their own frustrations.

You can model good behavior for them by not losing your cool or raising your voice in anger, no matter how much you might want to. If you can remain calm in the face of a preschooler in the middle of a meltdown, your demeanor may calm them down as well.

Reacting poorly yourself may encourage the child to throw more tantrums because it shows their behavior will elicit a response and they gain negative attention.

You may have to remove the child from the location if you have to, even it means leaving a full buggy of groceries at the front of the store. (You can say you will be back when your child has calmed down.) I have seen a few of these moments and many parents tell me that this strategy works well.

Here is a column I wrote on tantrums a few years ago that include a few more ideas, tools and strategies for coping (and for preventing and surviving) these negative but very typical outbursts.

Dear Ms. Barber:

Help! Every time I take my four-year-old shopping, she throws herself on the floor kicking and screaming until I buy her a toy or sugary treat that she is requesting from the shelves and again at the checkout. It is so embarrassing and I am tired of the stares and comments from the cashier and other customers as well as the vicious cycle we have developed.

~ Exasperated with tantrums!

Dear Exasperated:

Temper tantrums can be infuriating and embarrassing. Sometimes young children have tantrums because they are tired or hungry and parents are dragging them to places they don't have the skills or resources to handle.

Tantrums are a form of communication and your child could be sending a message that she is not able to cope with this outing and that she has needs that should be met. A well-rested child with a full stomach is a more pleasant companion on any shopping trip or outing.

Take along a favorite toy or healthy snack in a special bag for when the child "wants" something. I do not recommend giving in to the tantrum with the purchase of any new and "wanted" item. My mother used to prepare a list of groceries or items to purchase with my brother, sister, and me, including pictures from flyers and one "special" item for us to find at the end of the shopping trip.

Children love to assist in finding items on the shelves. Young children are also easily distracted and this is a valuable tool to use when your children are young. Remember to stay calm and respectful with your reactions and redirections, and remember that "this too shall pass."

One important point to remember is that your child's temper tantrums are not directed personally at you.

Tantrums typically occur between one and four years of age (a time in your child's development when they see themselves as the center of the universe), but older children can have tantrums as well. Between the ages of four and seven, it's not uncommon for children to yell, throw things, or just fall apart when they don't get what they want. In both of these stages, your child's tantrums are all about the perceived lack of control of their surroundings.

Try not to take these outbursts personally. While this may be difficult to do, remember, your child lacks the daily self-control that we adults take for granted. Temper tantrums are the only way your child knows how to express their frustrations with the world around them.

Here are a few strategies that can help you reduce or possibly eliminate the tantrums:

- Give your young child some control over her life. Many times children react negatively simply because they want a little more independence from you. From the time they wake up, begin giving them choices for little decisions such as whether they want a smoothie for breakfast or a bowl of cereal, or allowing them to choose their clothing and footwear for the day.

  One thing to avoid, however, is giving your child an open-ended option to do something, such as "Do you want to brush your teeth?" because the answer will almost always be "NO!" Instead, consider offering your child two options:

"Would you like to brush your teeth now or after you put your socks on?"

- Think of ways to distract your child. Young children have a very short attention span. The average three year old will change the focus of her attention approximately every minute, so you can use this to your advantage if you feel a tantrum brewing.

Before going out, bring a bag of distractions in case your child begins to squirm or reach for items you are not going to buy. When you feel a tantrum coming on, take something out of the "fun bag" and offer it to the child.

Examples can be a colorful notepad and bag of bright markers, a favorite interactive picture book, or when all else fails, a small healthy snack.

Remember to rotate these items regularly so that your child does not tire of them.

By also using a steady, cheerful and positive voice, you can distract your child from the object of her desire to finding the imaginary butterfly or ladybug that you just saw fly by.

Be creative, especially at this stage and age of development.

I hope in time that the tantrums will subside as your child learns, grows and develops self-regulation (the ability to stay calmly focused and alert, able to deal with strong emotions without the influence or help of others) along with your positive reinforcement, guidance and understanding. Good luck!

~ Ms. Barber

Never have more children than you have car windows.
~ Erma Bombeck

Chapter Three

Sibling Rivalries

Sibling Rivalry is a normal part of growing up, but it can drive parents crazy. What is the key to minimizing disputes at home? How do we know when to let our children work out their problems themselves and when to step in and play the referee?

I know from my own family experiences that brothers and sisters fight—it's just the natural ebb and flow of family life. I am the middle child of three and have an older brother and younger sister. I recall many moments of sibling rivalry and the stressors we put our parents through as well. I have researched and learned that different personalities and ages can play a role, but siblings also often see themselves as rivals, competing for an equal share of limited family resources (like the bathroom, telephone, or last piece of cake) and the attention of their parents.

Many different things can cause siblings to fight. Most brothers and sisters experience some degree of jealousy or competition, and this can flare into squabbles and bickering. But other factors also might influence how often kids fight and how severe the fighting gets. These include:

- **Evolving needs.** It's natural for children's changing needs, anxieties, and identities to affect how they relate to one another.

  For example, toddlers are naturally protective of their toys and belongings, and are learning to assert their will, which they'll do at every turn. If a baby brother or sister picks up the toddler's toy, the older child may react aggressively.

  School-age children often have a strong concept of fairness and equality, and might not understand why siblings of other ages are treated differently, or they may feel like one child gets different treatment.

  Teenagers, on the other hand, are developing a sense of individuality and independence, and might resent helping with household responsibilities, taking care of younger siblings, or even having to spend time together.

All of these differences can influence the way children fight with one another.

- **Individual temperaments.** Your children's individual temperaments—including mood, disposition, and adaptability—and their unique personalities play a large role in how well they get along. For example, if one child has an easy temperament and another is difficult, they may often have difficulties getting along. Similarly, a child who is especially sensitive, shy and drawn to parents for comfort and love might be resented by siblings who see this and want the same amount of attention. (In Chapter Twelve, I will define temperaments and explain the three typical dispositions.)

- **Special needs or children who are ill.** Sometimes, a child's special needs due to illness or learning/emotional exceptionalities may require more parental time, understanding and energy. Other children may pick up on this and act out to get attention or out of fear of what's happening to the other child.

- **Role models.** The way that parents resolve problems and disagreements sets a strong example for children.

If you and your partner or spouse work through conflicts in a way that's respectful, productive, and not aggressive, you increase the chances that your children will adopt those behaviors when they run into problems with one another. If your children see you routinely shout, slam doors, and loudly argue when you have problems, they're likely to pick up those negative habits themselves.

I am including a column I wrote on this subject and hope these additional tools and strategies will help you with the ups and downs of parenting multiple children.

Dear Ms. Barber:

Our two young girls (3½ and 5½ years of age) are always fighting over toys and other items in the house and it seems that they never get along.

I have read about sibling rivalry and we are very worried that they will never get along and be able to share. Please give us some ideas to try.

~ Seeking Sibling Harmony not Rivalry

Dear Seeking Harmony:

You are not alone and your experiences with your girls are very typical. All children go through developmental stages where at one stage they are almost incapable of sharing, to the next stage, when they finally develop an ability to share.

You have two young children in two different stages of development and this typically will cause stress and issues for all children when sharing is involved.

Preschool age siblings who are close in age may find themselves in constant conflict when it comes to sharing.

When at play, the younger child will have difficulty sharing and because of this the older child may become angry.

The issue isn't sibling rivalry or lack of love for one another. The issue is one where each child is at a different developmental level.

I have experienced that placing this type of behavior into a context of sibling rivalry only creates a problem where it doesn't have to exist.

One solution could be to explain to the older child that the younger hasn't yet learned to share.

The older child can be praised for having learned to share and can also be commended for having patience with the younger sibling until the skill of sharing has been learned.

Helping the older sibling place the issue in developmental terms helps release bad feelings the older child may have been feeling.

The sibling is no longer seen as bad, just younger and needing to learn. The older child can be encouraged to share toys with the younger sibling to help teach or role model how to share.

Now, instead of developing sibling rivalry, you are encouraging important life skills such as cooperation and understanding in the older child, thus helping to develop empathy, caring and self-regulation.

As for a younger sibling, the child can be encouraged by the parent to share and take turns with the toys.

Depending on the age of the younger child, it may be necessary for the parent to take the toy away and give it to the older child to have a turn, using a warm and caring tone.

It is important that the parent take this action and not the older child. The parent has legitimate authority to make the decision where the older child does not.

As well, in taking the toy from the younger child, the parent should tell the child, "Time to share... It's your brother's (or sister's) turn."

This will ensure that the play or use of the toy is a parental decision and not something the younger child can hold against the older child.

You may also want to use a timer for a two- to five-minute warning for sharing toys and other transitions that young children may struggle with during the early years.

As both children grow and develop, both will achieve cooperative play. You, the parent, will have encouraged empathy, cooperation and understanding in the older child and both may now come to share well between themselves without parental intervention.

Your children's relationship will remain intact. This is sibling harmony and a great path to a lifelong mutually supportive sibling relationship.

Years ago, I read a great book on sibling rivalry and would like to recommend it to all parents of multiples: *Siblings Without Rivalry: How to Help Your Children Live Together So You Can Live Too*, by Adele Faber and Elaine Mazlish.

~ *Ms. Barber*

Treat a child as though he already is the person he's capable of becoming.
~ Haim Ginott

Chapter Four

Nature vs. Electronics

Our world has changed drastically over the last few decades with technology and access to electronic media. Our children are all consumed with television, computers, movies, gaming equipment, social media and the Internet. Many parents have voiced their concerns with me that their children are spending countless hours in front of screens and on their gaming equipment instead of enjoying the fresh air and physical activities outside that my generation grew up with and thoroughly enjoyed for long periods of time.

The difference between my childhood and my twenty-on-year-old son's childhood is astonishing! This generation is so plugged into electronic diversions, especially with their phones, that it has lost its connection to the natural world and socially they are lacking important "people" skills when it comes to communicating and interacting face to face.

My memories of growing up include many hours spent "out of doors" every day, after school, after dinner, and on weekends.

We could not get enough time outside with our friends and family enjoying hikes, cycling, walking, playing and exploring with nature. Our parents struggled with getting us to come back inside and television was a limited "treat."

Times have certainly changed!

My advice to parents, once again, is to model the appropriate behaviors and actions we want our children to learn and develop for themselves.

Some parents not only model a preoccupation with staring at screens, but they encourage it as well. I have observed many parents with young children at a restaurant or sitting in a public area and their children are using an electronic gadget as a pacifier. Even while children are in their company, parents are all-consumed by having to respond to a text message within seconds or taking a phone call while engaged with their children.

How then can they expect their children to resist the attraction of electronic devices? How can they set limits for children when it is so hard for them to do as well? It is almost impossible to help our children learn how to self-monitor and set limits without being committed to the idea ourselves.

Even when we are aware of the effects of screen time on ourselves and our children, it is difficult to break this habit. I encourage you to keep at it and to monitor the amount of time your family is spending in front of screens. This includes watching television, playing on phones or iPad, using the computer, or playing video games.

Try to establish a "screen-free" time for a few hours each evening so you can eat dinner together and play a family game inside or outside.

For this chapter, I am including a column in response to a mother "concerned with new generation of electronic play." Chapter Nine also includes some great ideas for eating meals together as a family, my personal experiences with my family meals, and a few tips for picky eaters.

Dear Ms. Barber:

I am enjoying your column thoroughly and have a question for you regarding television, electronics and computers for children under five years of age.

So many parents today complain that their kids are always inside and plugged in to something electronic and that they never play outside with their friends like we used to when we were growing up.

I am worried for my little children and wondered if you have any suggestions or research on this subject!
~ Mother Concerned With New Generation of Electronic Play

Dear Mother Concerned:

You have every right to be concerned for your children and all of the others who are spending most of their free time indoors and "plugged in" to something electronic.

I recently read the book *Last Child in the Woods: Saving Our Children from Nature-Deficit Disorder*, by Richard Louv, and highly recommend it to all parents and educators who are struggling with a generation lacking in direct exposure to nature.

In his book, Louv details studies and research on the growing body of evidence linking the lack of nature and increase in time spent with electronics in children's lives, and the rise in childhood obesity, attention disorders, and depression.

Swedish researchers compared children within two early childhood care settings: at one, television and computers were readily available and the outdoor play space was limited and made of steel, plastic and other man-made materials.

At the second center, electronics were limited and rarely available and the outdoor play area was based on an "outdoors in all weather" natural theme. The children enjoyed playing with a variety of natural materials two to three times a day.

Those children attending the second center had better motor coordination, more ability to concentrate, less agitation and irritation, less impulsive behavior and greater creativity. The researchers found that direct exposure to nature was essential for a child's healthy physical and emotional development.

Those attending the first center had difficulty with attention span and struggled with impulsive behavior and irritability. Sleep disturbances were also noticed.

I recommend adding nature activities and outdoor adventures to your everyday daily routines with your young children and limiting the time they spend with television and computer/video games.

I understand that time is precious and our lives are full of schedules and commitments. You may be pleasantly surprised that your children will sleep better after an evening of fresh air and may respond more positively after they experience joy and wonder from outdoor activities with simple natural materials instead of an afternoon or evening in front of the television.

You may also find that your time spent out-of-doors will also help "clear your mind" and improve your emotional well-being as well.

I am thankful for the reminder of my active and fun childhood and the wonderful times I spent exploring in nature with my family and friends.

~ Ms. Barber

Parents need to fill a child's bucket of self-esteem so high that the rest of the world cannot poke enough holes to drain it dry.
~ Alvin Price

Chapter Five

Self-Esteem and Raising Confident Children

By definition, self-esteem is the way in which an individual perceives herself, in other words, her own thoughts and feelings about herself and her ability to achieve in ways that are important to her. Our children's self-esteem is shaped not only by their own perceptions and expectations, but also by the perceptions and expectations of the important people in their life. It is connected to how they are thought of and treated by parents, teachers and friends.

The closer a child's perceived self (how she sees herself) comes to her ideal self (how she would like to be), the higher a child's self-esteem will be.

Dear Ms. Barber:

Our child has just turned 5 years old and is starting to make negative comments about her abilities and has become stressed and anxious every time we leave the house for soccer practice.

She is going into kindergarten in the fall and has a number of fears. We are worried about her developing low self-esteem and not doing well in school. She is not very outgoing and is somewhat shy and reserved in new situations.

We are concerned that she will develop into an anxious and fearful person if we don't help her now.

Do you have any advice, ideas or experience with children like our daughter?
~ Anxious About Anxiety and
Stress in Our Child

Dear Anxious:

Yes, I have met and taught many children who are "slow-to-warm up" in temperament and have a more reserved personality.

We all have differences in the ways we react, respond and relate to our environments and to the people we meet and every child is so diverse and different.

Your child is typical, and many young children experience low self-esteem, anxiety and fearfulness for a variety of reasons.

Over the years I have observed and personally experienced that most of our stress, anxiety and fearfulness is due in part because we expect a negative outcome.

Children are typically hopeful by nature and can be quickly and easily influenced by our adult anxiety, stress and fears and "pick up" on our emotions.

Paying attention to our thoughts and expectations and "sprinkling" them with optimism can reduce anxiety, stress and fear in our young children.

I have learned that leading by example, and being more positive and confident in the choice of words and statements, can help to raise optimistic children who are less fearful and anxious, and we can even change our own lives in the process as well.

Dr. Lynne Kenney has developed a list of strategies to encourage optimism in our children and I have included her ideas for you to practice.

1. Help your children set themselves up for success. Participating in jobs or tasks, activities and physical sports that are within your children's abilities will provide them with positive experiences, increasing their self-esteem and allowing them to see themselves as capable.

2. Give specific feedback on what your child does well. Instead of offering general praise, be specific. "You practiced so many multiplication problems that you earned an A on your recent test." "Your effort and practice earn you better grades."

3. Validate their feelings, offering some strategies for looking more hopefully at the circumstances. "It didn't feel very good to miss the goal at soccer, but your footwork on the field was excellent. Daddy and I will play more with you in the backyard so you are better prepared for the next time."

4. Use positive not negative labels. Negative labels lead children to believe they are the label. So use positive labels when talking with and about your child.

As an example, when your child exhibits a behavior that is unsuitable such as whining, refrain from calling your child a "whiner" and practice using a new tone with your child.

"Sara, when you ask for what you want in a positive tone, I can respond better to you. Let's use a happy tone as we talk with one another."

5. Comment on the bright side. "I know it's raining so we must play indoors; this is our chance to make a huge train station today."

For healthy self-esteem, our children need to develop, achieve and acquire some or all of the following characteristics:

A Sense of Belonging

Young children need to feel loved and accepted for who they are by others, beginning with their immediate family and then extending out to other groups such as friends, sports team mates, childcare and schoolmates, a church or temple, and even their neighbourhood or community.

Children without this sense of acceptance or group identity, may feel rejected, lonely, and adrift without a "family", "group" or "home."

A Sense of Security

Children must feel secure about themselves and their future.

A Sense of Purpose

Children should have goals that give them purpose and great direction along with an avenue for channeling their endless energy and curiosity toward achievement and positive self-expression.

If they lack a sense of purpose, they may feel bored, aimless, and even resentful at being pushed in certain directions by you or others involved in their growth and development.

A Sense of Personal Competence and Pride

Your children should feel confident in their ability to meet any challenges in their lives. Having successful life experiences in solving problems independently, being creative and getting results for their efforts will give them a sense of personal power and inner confidence.

Setting appropriate expectations, not too low and not too high, is critical to developing competence and confidence. If you are overprotecting them, and if they are too dependent on you, or if expectations are so high they never succeed, they may feel powerless and incapable of controlling the circumstances in their lives.

A Sense of Family Self-esteem

Your child's self-esteem initially develops within the family and is influenced greatly by the feelings and perceptions that a family has of itself.

This philosophy of mine is based on many years of practical experience with children, from my own childhood with my family and upbringing, my trial and error approach to parenting my son, and from all of the research and theories I have studied and taught within my ECE college classroom.

Family pride is essential to self-esteem and can be nourished and maintained in many ways, including participation or involvement in your community through age-appropriate activities, tracing a family's heritage and ancestors with a family tree, or caring for extended family members.

Families succeed and flourish when members focus on each other's strengths, avoid excessive negative criticism and support each other outside of the family setting. Family members should believe in each other, respect individual differences and show their affection for each other. Make time for being together, whether it is to enjoy special events, share holiday traditions or just to have fun.

Enjoy each other every day and love each other unconditionally.

~Ms Barber

Raising optimistic children begins with you. Seeing the positive side of life experiences, learning from mishaps and practicing positive thoughts, leads to happier children."
~ Martin Seligman, author
The Optimistic Child

You can't control how some people will treat you or what they'll say about you. But you can control how you react to it.
~ Author Unknown

Chapter Six

Self-Regulation

Are your children aware of their feelings, needs, and impulses? Can they calm themselves, control their behavior, and focus on tasks? Preschoolers who can do these things find it easier to take turns, make friends, and adapt to school routines. This emotional/social ability is called "self-regulation."

Self-regulation is a deep, internal mechanism that enables children as well as adults to engage in mindful, intentional, and thoughtful behaviors. It has two sides: firstly, it involves the ability to control one's impulses and to stop doing something, such as pushing a friend out of a line up to wash hands for snack time. Secondly, self-regulation involves the capacity to do something (even if one doesn't want to do it) because it is needed, such as waiting one's turn.

Self-regulated children can delay gratification and suppress their immediate impulses enough to think ahead to the possible consequences of their actions or to consider alternative actions that would be more appropriate.

While most children know that they are supposed to "use their words" instead of fighting, only children who have acquired a level of self-regulation are actually able to use them.

Teaching young children self-regulation first requires strong parent and caregiver self-regulation. Children learn to regulate thoughts, feelings, behavior, and emotion by watching and responding to adults' self-regulation.

Ellen Galinsky is president and co-founder of the Families and Work Institute, and author of the best-selling *Mind in the Making: The Seven Essential Life Skills Every Child Needs* and *The Six Stages of Parenthood*. Referring to motivational regulation, Galinsky notes, "Adults foster children's motivation by being motivated themselves" (2010, 11). Parents and caregivers of young children play a vital role in helping children develop foundational self-regulation skills.

Fortunately, young children's everyday experiences offer abundant opportunities for developing self-regulation. Parents can take advantage of these opportunities by

- identifying each child's developmental stage and planning the kinds of modeling, hints, and cues the child needs to continue his or her development;

- withdrawing direct support as children begin to demonstrate new skills; and

- monitoring children's activities to ensure they are successful.

When parents and caregivers deliberately teach self-regulation as part of everyday experiences, they help children become actively engaged learners, laying the foundation for years of future success in school and life.

I have found through practical experience with children under five years of age, that self-regulation is the foundation of early learning, social competence, emotional maturity, physical skills and well-being. By the time children are four- and five-year-olds, basic voluntary regulatory systems are established. Children now can intentionally attend and adapt to situations. I have observed that self-regulation supports children's growing abilities to think about their feelings and to represent these feelings, intentions and actions in their words, play, drawings and block constructions. Children need opportunities to practice the tools of self-regulation in everyday situations and learn strategies from first-hand actions with objects in their world, and from exchanging points of view with peers and adults.

I have included my column on self-regulation to offer more tips and tools for all involved in the growth and development of early learners and to offer a few more strategies and ideas for nurturing young children.

Dear Ms. Barber:

I am a retired teacher, mother of two and grandmother of four, and I have attended your StrongStart center regularly.

I am enjoying reading your column and advice and want to comment on the column, "Preparing for kindergarten," from Tuesday, March 29, and I would like to ask if you could give parents suggestions and ideas for helping their children to develop self-regulation skills.

We spoke on this topic once in your classroom as you have posters giving examples and ideas on this topic. I feel that many parents and grandparents should have this information to assist and support their preschoolers with practice in developing these much needed skills and abilities for kindergarten and future life.

I agree with your statement, "helping your child 'get ready' for kindergarten is not a competition."

Keep up the great work, Ms. Barber.

~ A Very Thankful Grandparent

Dear Thankful Grandparent:

Thank you for your kind words. Self-regulation is a mixture of social and emotional behaviors and the development of skills that can be a life-long challenge for many individuals.

By definition, "Self-regulation is the ability to adapt one's emotions, behaviors and attention to the demands of the situation. It is also known as internal motivation for adapting to, and understanding, emotional and social demands." These skills are essential for successful transition to school environments.

Self-regulation has often been called self-control or self-direction and involves children's capacity for controlling emotions, interacting in positive ways with others, and avoiding inappropriate or aggressive actions.

The posters in my classroom list self-regulation skills simply as: the ability to take turns and waiting for a turn, sharing ideas, problem solving, managing strong emotions, planning ahead and planning with others, getting along with others, using a number of strategies to reach a goal, and struggling through the hard bits to learn something new.

These are skills and abilities that are very important for children to practice before entering kindergarten and the same skills that they will work to develop throughout their early school years. They are also important skills that all adults can model for the children in their lives.

As mentioned in my previous column, preparing children for kindergarten is really about helping your child develop in a well-rounded way in all areas of development through play, practice, exploration and positive encouragement.

Years ago, I read a very good book on this subject by Lawrence J. Cohen. The book is called *Playful Parenting*, and Cohen explains the value of being a playful parent, the importance of connecting with your child's emotions and accepting strong feelings (theirs and yours) and how to support self-control and self-regulation with all members of your family and with others in your environment.

As I mentioned in my last column, we are very fortunate to have many resources, organizations and early childhood specialists in many of our communities. Locally, I will add Penticton and District Childcare Resource Services (PDCRS) and Communities for Kids to the list of valuable resources for parents and caregivers. If you live elsewhere, look for similar resources near you.

Remember to give your children positive support and lots of opportunities to play, practice and explore with age-appropriate materials and other children.

~ Ms. Barber

Our children are counting on us to provide two things: consistency and structure.

~ Barbara Coloroso

Bedtime: the perfect time for children to ask multiple questions, require more food and drinks, require additional bathroom breaks, and request a new nightlight.
~ Author Unknown

Chapter Seven

Bedtime Routines

I have heard from many parents over the years that they couldn't resist their little one's pleas for "Just ten more minutes" of his favorite TV show, storybook, computer game, or outdoor play activity and now bedtime has come and gone. They would turn off the television, computer, and/or call him inside and pull out his pajamas and whisk him upstairs to his room. They had no time to read or wind down. But he's very tired, so he'll sleep, right? Well, not exactly.

"Everyone needs a series of predictable steps that they take every night to help them sleep," says Jill Spivack, a sleep specialist and co-creator of *The Sleepeasy Solution* and momlogic.com.

In other words, whisking him from playtime to bedtime might actually be depriving your child of the very cues he needs to make it smoothly into slumber. The good news: a solid routine can make evenings less stressful and far more fun for everyone.

I have developed a few strategies of my own from parenting a son and have developed a few more over the years of researching and working with exhausted parents. Sleep training of any kind helps parents learn how to offer valuable and much needed support to their children as they are learning to sleep and to prepare for bedtime. I am a firm believer in regular bedtime and naptime routines for children under five years of age. Actually, we could all benefit from regular sleep patterns and rest as I have found to be true this past year of my life and my battle with inflammatory breast cancer. Yes, I fought and won the battle and I am so pleased for this new lease on life and wonderful new chapter in my life.

The solution I have found that has worked for me and countless other parents is to make bedtime a priority, A very predictable, calming experience and routine that is the key to a great night's sleep. No matter what age you are, we all need a calming experience to soothe away the day and go easy into a peaceful sleep.

My favorite band, The Eagles, sing a song titled "Peaceful, Easy Feeling." This is exactly what we all need in our lives. I have encouraged and supported the love of my life to adopt my philos-ophy on having a soothing bath routine before bed a few times a week. It certainly helps to calm and soothe away the events of the day and helps to prepare the mind, body and soul for a restful, peaceful and easy sleep. You can add lavender oil, small amounts of aromatherapy, Epsom salts or bubbles, and play soothing music to help calm the mind and feed the soul.

Whatever strategy you choose for your child and family members is up to you, but please avoid active play and electronic devices, which research states is very stimulating for the brain of all ages.

Some wonderful bedtime ideas and routines from parents I have worked with include: giving your child a bath as I mentioned earlier, reading stories to your child as he cuddles in your lap, and saying a few prayers for loved ones and friends. While cuddling, you could praise your child for a specific accomplishment and talk about his day. If you play bedtime music, always choose soothing and quiet choices and then tuck your child into bed and say good night. I used to say to my son, "Sweet dreams, sweet boy."

Experiment to find out what works best for you and your child and once you settle into a positive routine, follow it consistently every night. Children need consistent and predictable routines and guidance.

Another problem that parents have shared with me is that they are tired of the whining at bedtime and give up and let their children fall asleep in front of the television or in their bed.

I understand that bedtime battles can test the patience and understanding of most parents. It is so important to hang in there and not give up or give in. Be patient and try a few of these ideas and strategies and eventually you will have a successful bedtime routine.

It is never too late to teach and guide your children into good sleeping habits and patterns. If your child is pushing the limits, as most do, state your expectations in your loving and caring manner and stick to the routine. Eventually, your consistency and warm, caring attitude will pay off in a great night's sleep for everyone.

I wrote a column on sleep habits and bedtime routines and have included it here as well, as another resource for you.

Dear Ms. Barber:

My friends and I all have children under the age of four and we all have different ideas on the amount of sleep our children should experience each night and what time they should go to bed.

We also have trouble with bedtime routines and wonder if you could help with ideas on how to get our children to go to bed, stay in their beds and have a full night's sleep.

~Sleepless with Preschoolers in the House

Dear Sleepless:

Research states that preschoolers should sleep about 10 to 12 hours during each 24-hour period.

The most important tip I can give you is that you must help your children develop good habits for getting to sleep and provide consistency and regular routines for greatest success.

I recommend that you pick—and stick to—a set bedtime each night. If possible, try to put your child to bed at the same time every night, ideally at 7:30 or 8 p.m.

This will help your child's internal clock stay on track and make it easier for her to fall asleep easily and quickly at bedtime.

Staying up too late or going to bed at a different time each night will cause your preschooler to become overtired.

This also makes it harder for her to settle down and get to sleep, and the next day you may have an irritable and easily frustrated child to manage.

As I mentioned earlier, it is important to develop a consistent bedtime routine for young children. A bedtime routine is a great way to ensure that your preschooler is getting enough sleep.

Here are a few suggestions to keep in mind when establishing a bedtime routine:

- Include a winding-down period during the half hour before bedtime without any exercise or physical activities.

- Always prepare your child with a warning at half an hour and ten minutes beforehand. Children of this age range need a warning time to transition from one activity to the next.

- Always avoid stimulants, such as food and drinks with caffeine and sugar near bedtime. You would be amazed at how many children's drinks and snacks have caffeine in them.

- Many childcare specialists encourage making the bedroom a quiet, cozy and special place that is conducive to sleeping.

- Your child's bed should be used only for sleeping—not for playing on, jumping on or watching TV from, and most specialists will discourage you from having a TV in your young child's bedroom. Television stimulates young children's minds and this will interfere with sleeping and bedtime.

- Allow your child choices for a smooth transition, such as which pajamas to wear, stuffed animal to take to bed, story to read, etc.

- Include three or four soothing activities, such as taking a bath, changing into warm pajamas fresh from the clothes dryer, and reading bedtime stories, etc.

- Consider playing soft, soothing music or choose a story with sleeping and bedtime as the theme.

- Tuck your child into bed snugly for a feeling of security and try to anticipate all of your child's requests and include them in his nightly routine.

Your young child may start trying to put off bedtime by manipulating and whining for "just one more" story, song, glass of water, hug, and so on.

Instead of growing more exasperated, try to anticipate all of her usual, but reasonable requests and make them part of the bedtime routine.

Then allow your child one extra request and make it clear that one is the limit. Your child will feel like she is getting her way, but you will know that you are getting yours!

It is also important for young children to get outside for fresh air and exercise each day.

This will also help to ensure that your child will be tired at the end of the day and ready to fall asleep.

Lastly and most importantly, please remember that reading books before bedtime encourages the emotional connection parents can achieve by cuddling up and reading a great story with their children.

Parents can create a bedtime routine that promotes the joy of reading, importance of early literacy habits and a warm, loving environment where closeness is nurtured.

Hopefully you will start to experience a smoother and more enjoyable bedtime routine for you and your young children.

~Ms. Barber

If you tell the truth, you don't have to remember anything.

~ Mark Twain

No matter what I do, my mom can always tell when I'm lying.
~ Jeff, age 8

Chapter Eight

Telling Tall Tales

There's a great cartoon that I have seen on social media from time to time. "He did that," says the young blue crayon character, pointing to his red crayon friend. The two crayons are being brought to task in front of a green parent crayon character. There's a glitch in the blue crayon's argument, though. The drawing all over the walls is blue.

Most, if not all, parents will relate to it. My parents certainly can as they raised three colorful crayons.

The irony in this funny cartoon is that many parents' response to their children's tall tales does little more than to encourage it, say experts.

"If you are too harsh, too unforgiving and too controlling, you create an air of anxiety in your home and an air of perfection that may be stress-ful," explains parenting coach Sue Atkins.

Other parents quite literally set their children up to lie by asking questions about something they've done wrong, to which they already know the answer, she adds. The better response would be to name what they've done, rather than try and trap them into providing information that they know will lead them straight into trouble.

I have experienced and researched this topic on many occasions for parents and have found that it is also important to remember that very young children simply don't understand the difference between what "telling the truth" is and what isn't.

Many early learning experts call this "healthy lying" as it involves innocent fantasy and imagination, which is important in the development of children. To discipline them for their creative thoughts and imagination will only confuse them.

Preschool children (aged three to five) are learning to grasp the line between reality and fantasy. Telling a fib or tall tale is not an unusual way to explore this boundary at this age. Parents are often quick to react in an angry way to what they see as a lie. But this may not always be the best way to handle the situation.

I have had many parents of preschoolers say to me, "Oh my gosh, my child is lying. I don't know what to do." Lying causes anxiety and unrest in many parents' lives and they want their children to be honest and to have good morals.

If your three-year-old spilled milk on the floor, you would ask, "Who spilled it?" and your child might say, "Not me." It's not that your child is lying. She may wish she didn't spill it, or if the spill took place an hour ago, she might not even remember spilling it.

Pediatric psychologist Mark Bowers states that anyone under age five is too young to understand what a lie is. They don't have the same cognitive capacity as a kindergarten-age child who begins to learn the difference between right and wrong.

"You don't have a future criminal on your hands because your child's not 'fessing up to spilling the milk in the kitchen," Bowers says.

If you catch your child drawing on the walls, you may be tempted to confront her: "Are you the one who did this?" Chances are she'll say "no" because she doesn't want to make you mad or get in trouble.

It's better to state what the rule is and offer a solution, Bowers says. For example, "We have a rule in this house that we only draw on paper. So why don't we get some soap and you can help Daddy clean it up."

To avoid accusations, he advocates a Columbo approach, or playing dumb. Within your child's earshot, you can say: "Oh, I wonder how this milk got spilled? It would really be nice if somebody could help me clean it up."

After your child comes over and helps you, give him a high-five for helping out.

These are teaching opportunities that show your child what they should do in the future, and I refer to them as "teachable moments" that will assist your child in the development of problem solving and other important life skills for the future. In Chapter Eleven, I will also help to remind and explain the role of the parent as a child's first teacher and the importance of developing a positive and nurturing environment and relationship that encourages honesty and open communication.

I have raised my son with this philosophy and style of communication and parenting and kept the connections open so that he could tell me anything without judgment and attacks on his character. I have to admit that there were times in middle school and high school when I had moments where I had thought that it might be better that I did not have all of the information and facts. But I am thankful and proud that he could come to me with important questions and concerns and that he felt supported and loved unconditionally to share "the whole truth, and nothing but the truth."

I wrote a column on this topic as well and have included it in this chapter to give other ideas, strategies and tools on how to handle and understand lies and untruths in the preschool stage of development.

Dear Ms. Barber:

Our preschooler is starting to tell lies and untruths. At first we thought it was funny and cute that he was living in the fantasy world and recalling "stories" to family members about riding a dragon and catching the Easter Bunny in our yard. Now, he has started to lie about important things in our everyday lives and we are worried. Is this normal for this age group?

~Worried About Tall Tales

Dear Worried About Tall Tales:

Most children under age six often tell "fibs" and "little white lies" and have difficulty distinguishing between fantasy and reality. Telling "tall tales" is entirely different from lying and can be an expression of your child's creative imagination at work, and researchers tell us that it is a key achievement in your child's cognitive development.

I have experienced and researched that lying is quite common in preschoolers. Children in this age group often don't yet understand that lying is wrong and dishonest. Because of this, parents should not discipline their preschoolers for lying.

Instead, parents should, when their children lie, use the occasions as teachable moments. When their preschooler tells lies, parents should take the opportunity to teach their child why lying is wrong. Preschoolers generally tell two kinds of lies:

Tall tales
Tall tales are when a child makes up a story that isn't true, or greatly exaggerates something that is true.

Children in this stage have vivid imaginations, and are just learning to know the difference between fantasy and reality. When children tell tall tales, they're often expressing things that they wish were true.

When children tell tall tales, parents can do two things. First, they can simply listen to their children's stories and leave it at that.

Second, parents can try to interject some reality into their children's stories.

For example, if a child says something like, "I can eat 100 hotdogs for dinner," a parent could reply, "You wish you could eat that many, don't you?"

Lies to get something they want, or to avoid something they don't want

Preschoolers tell these types of lies for the same reasons that adults do, but they often don't see anything wrong with telling a lie to gain a result they want.

When children in this stage tell these types of lies, parents should try not to overreact. Instead, they should point out to their children that it is wrong to lie, and that it is important to tell the truth.

Even though preschoolers don't generally know that lying is wrong, this is a good time for parents to start teaching them the basics of telling the truth. A good place for parents to start is by letting their children know how happy it makes them when their children tell the truth, and that not telling the truth makes it hard for them to develop trust.

I have researched a few of the causes and have found a child's lying may be the result of numerous factors. These can include:

- fear of disappointing a parent,

- avoiding punishment,

- seeking attention,

- crying out for help,

- avoiding stressful situations, and

- imitating the behavior of the adults around him.

Remember to model truthfulness. Children learn by watching their parents. Parents who lie to their children and in their children's presence are teaching their children that lying is an acceptable behavior. Parents should try to set a good example for their children by being as truthful as possible themselves.

Always praise truthfulness. Parents should make every effort to praise their children when they are being honest. I have learned over the years that behavior that is praised is much more likely to be repeated.

~ Ms. Barber

Chapter Nine

Food for Thought: Beefs and Bouquets

I have had many discussions with parents over the years regarding family dinners and the lack there-of and have had many questions surrounding eating habits and food refusals among toddlers and preschoolers.

As I write this chapter, I am reminded of a very special memory from my childhood and all of the wonderful family dinners that I have shared with my parents, siblings and extended family members.

My mother always had a delicious home-cooked meal ready for my hard-working father, and my brother, sister and I would look forward to sharing our day with my parents and with each other at the dinner table.

I will never forget the endless laughter, great food and amazing conversations about every topic under the sun.

One Sunday, during a family dinner, my mother asked my siblings and me to share one positive comment about each family member and she called this a "bouquet."

She also asked if we had anything negative we needed to discuss with any member and this would be known forever as the "beef."

From that day forward we would refer to these conversations, problem solving moments and wonderful times of sharing around the dinner table as the "Beef and Bouquet" time. She even brought this amazing time and memory to her speech at my brother's wedding in 1985 and encouraged him and his new wife to hopefully continue on this tradition of eating meals and sharing together with his future family.

I truly miss those days and special dinners with my family. Times have certainly changed and our lives have become very busy with schedules and commitments and so many distractions that keep us from sharing and eating meals together at the family table.

I am hearing from many families that their schedules are so tight and traditional sit-down, home-cooked meals with all members aren't realistic.

In the end, family meals are about more than food. When the family can sit and eat together— whether it is leftovers, takeout, or home-cooked meals—children benefit. Mealtimes matter.

I have found that eating together as a family is more important today than in the past because there are more competing distractions, more choices of activities outside the home, and a constant bombardment of information from modern technology. During the day most of us are out in the community mixing with all kinds of people. Our children are learning about the world from many sources, often without parental filters or input. Even when everyone is home, individuals do their own thing. Perhaps the only opportunity of the day to talk with each other is at the dinner table.

I had a parent write to me regarding her two-year-old daughter and the struggles they were having with a fussy, picky eater at mealtime. I shared my experiences and research on this subject with her in my column so that other parents could also read and learn that this topic and problem is very typical with most toddlers and preschoolers, including my son.

Dear Ms. Barber:

We are the proud parents of a two-year-old. Our toddler used to be an easy going infant and loved to eat anything and everything put in front of her and now she is the exact opposite. She is a very fussy, picky eater that refuses to eat and is very disruptive at our scheduled mealtimes.

I have read many books on the subject and just wanted to hear some new advice from you on her challenging behavior.

I really miss the harmony we used to have at mealtimes and wonder if I should be worried about the refusal of food.

~ Seeking Help for My Fussy, Picky Eater

Dear Parent of Fussy, Picky Eater:

Research and experience tells us that children have three basic temperaments within their personality: easy, slow-to-warm-up, and difficult.

The ways in which they relate and respond may vary and change from one stage to another and the shift to toddlerhood comes with the constant seeking of independence.

When any child doesn't eat as expected, nurturing parents find themselves very distressed.

I have heard from many parents that they have lost sleep and feel inadequate due to the picky eater tipping the balance of their family harmony. You are not alone.

Richard Canfield, a professor of human development at Cornell University, describes the behavior change in the early years as so fundamental and profound that he thinks of children at each new stage as a different species. I tend to agree with his findings.

After the age of six months, there is a rapid and dramatic shift in mealtime dynamics. In less than a year, babies move from total dependence on parents to self-feeding. Babies rarely refuse food, while toddlers delight in saying NO to just about everything, especially food.

Canfield describes toddlers as "motors without pilots." This may help to explain why mealtimes with toddlers are so challenging.

Most preschoolers (three- to five-year-olds) are more open to new experiences, and sometimes this includes food. As a child moves from one stage of development to the next one, the strategies required to achieve more pleasant meal-times change as well.

Never ask a toddler if he wants to eat. Simply announce that it is time to eat. Offer a variety of healthy and safe (choking-free) finger foods from each food group, find a healthy "dip" that she likes to eat, and allow her to dip everything.

You would be amazed at what toddlers will eat if it is "dipped" in their favorite dip. My son used to dip everything in ranch dressing.

Positive redirection and distraction with a sense of humor can also diffuse fussy, picky eaters and encourage them to eat what has been offered or bring them back to the task at hand: eating!

I have met many creative parents over the years and have learned through my own experience as well, that helping toddlers to recognize hunger can also be challenging.

Spacing out meals and snacks so that they are two or more hours apart allows young children to experience mild hunger, the satisfaction from eating and the need for eating.

Linda Piette, author of *Just Two More Bites!*, has developed a set of feeding guidelines for parents of toddlers and I have included a few for you:

- encourage the independence of self-feeding,

- be a good role model and eat with your child,

- give small portions to start and encourage your child to ask for more, and

- talk about being hungry or full.

She reminds that we should never ignore food throwing and recommends that we never insist that our children "clean their plates"; always start with small portions to avoid battles. She also warns that young children often fill up on liquids and become full and will then refuse to eat.

Even though picky eating is a passing phase for most children, there are exceptions. Some children have more complex needs and this is true when a child is not gaining weight or not eating like other children of the same age.

Regardless of the cause, a better understanding of your child's developmental needs will offer insights into how best to handle food refusals.

Seek out other parents and compare "notes," and talk to professionals and specialists such as nutritionists, dieticians, public health nurses and early childhood educators if you are concerned that your child is not developing at a healthy rate.

According to researchers, the majority of complaints about picky eating coincide with the time that a child's growth slows down and he begins to establish independence.

Finally, I want to remind all parents that you should never use food as a reward, punishment, or bribe and remember to make meal time and food choices feel like an adventure rather than a chore.

Good luck on your adventures in eating!

~ Ms. Barber

Consequences that are logically related to the behavior help teach children responsibility.
~ Ms. Barber

Chapter Ten

To Spank or Not to Spank?
That is the Question ...

The idea behind parental discipline is to ultimately create self-discipline within your child. That means that the child has to learn something—your value system, the difference between right and wrong and that you love him unconditionally—that will guide him or her throughout life.

As I mentioned in Chapter Six, self-regulation is the foundation of early learning, social competence, emotional maturity, physical skills and well-being. As parents, it is our responsibility to nurture and support this very important aspect of development and set of skills children will need to be effective and successful in school and in their future life.

What do children learn from being spanked? The swatting or hitting itself doesn't teach them anything positive. Whether you believe in physical punishment or not, I have researched healthy and positive techniques for managing children's behavior and alternatives to spanking and have also included some very important questions you need to ask yourself.

- Never take out your frustrations while spanking.

    Ask yourself if the spanking is truly warranted because of the child's behavior, or whether it's an excuse for you to have an adult temper tantrum.

    Are you more prone to spank when you are in an angry or bad mood?

- There needs to be a sense of calmness and order in the house.

    If you are spanking your child for being physical and chaotic, aren't you adding to the physical chaos by being physical and violent with your child?

    What are you teaching them?

Make a commitment to your child's discipline. You have to do what you say you're going to do. Consequences should be highly predictable for your child and easily understood. Children need limits and boundaries and deserve explanations and reasons for them.

As Dr. Phil states, "Define your child's currency. What does he or she value?" You can withdraw a positive (take away a favorite toy) or introduce a negative (giving a time-away) event—but always be consistent.

Develop a child-level logic. For example, children know that you are less likely to discipline them in public, so that is where they might act out and misbehave. Preschoolers need constant reminders of rules and behaviors before you go out. This is very important for this age group and stage of childhood development.

Two statements you should NEVER say to your child if you want him or her to behave are:

1. "I'll give you something to cry about," and

2. "Wait until your father gets home."

Children can see through your idle threats and will eventually ignore them. They will also take advantage of the fact that one parent doesn't want to deal with managing behavior and discipline and tries to hand it over to the other parent.

As I have mentioned previously, I have had many years of experience working with children and raising my own son, along with being raised by my positive and wonderful mother who was the best model for parenting. She taught me that giving children choices is an effective alternative to spanking.

If your child is playing with her food at the table, ask "Are you hungry and want to finish eating your food or would you like to leave the table?" If your child continues to play with her food and not eat it, then use kind but firm action by helping her down from the table. Tell her that she can return to the table when she is ready to eat her food and not play with it.

I have also learned that children respond very well to logical consequences.

Consequences that are logically related to the behavior help teach children responsibility. For example, your child breaks a neighbor's window and you punish him by spanking him. What does he learn about the situation? He may learn to never do that again, but he also learns that he needs to hide his mistakes, blame it on someone else, lie, or simply not get caught. I call this behavior "going underground," and I have seen it often with many children, but especially within the preteen and teen years. Your child may also develop a low sense of self-esteem and feel that he is bad or feel anger and revenge toward the parent who spanked him.

Research states that when you spank a child, he may only behave because he is afraid to get hit again and feel these negative thoughts about you and himself. He also learns that when you are angry it is okay to hit another person. Do you want your child to behave because he is afraid of you, or because he respects you?

Compare that situation to a child who breaks a neighbor's window and his parent says, using a kind but firm tone of voice, "I see you've broken the window. What will you do to repair it?" The child decides to mow the neighbor's lawn and wash his car several times to repay the cost of breaking the window.

What does the child learn in this situation? That mistakes are an inevitable part of life and it isn't so important that he made the mistake but that he takes responsibility to repair the mistake. The focus is taken off the mistake and behavior and put on taking responsibility for repairing it and learning that accidents happen. The child feels no anger or revenge toward his parent. And most importantly the child's self-esteem is not damaged.

I have included my column on spanking from a concerned parent of a three-year-old who was raised in a home where physical discipline and spanking was typical. In Chapter Eleven, Parents: A Child's First Teacher, I will explain how important it is to "make peace with your past," and break any habits you have formed from your experiences with your own childhood and parents, so as not to continue a negative cycle.

Many of my college students have read the book *Making Peace with Your Past*, written by H. Norman Wright in 1984. This book was also recommended to me while I was studying early childhood education in college and it changed my life.

Some of my students have also shared with me that they have grown and developed emotional intelligence because of this book along with the knowledge and research from our many lectures and lessons throughout their training with me. I highly recommend it to any parent or young adult who is reflecting on their events of the past that may have had a significant impact on their current behavior, habits and thoughts. These could include our relationships from our childhood or pressures and stressors from recent years that we need to make peace with and move forward with healthier and happier habits, actions and thoughts

Calm parents = calm children.

Dear Ms. Barber:

I was raised in a home where spanking and physical discipline was the norm and was the only way of disciplining. I recall how I felt all those years ago and still have negative feelings about the treatment I had from my parents. Now, as a parent of a three-year-old, I am embarrassed to say that I have spanked my child a few times and my husband has as well. Our toddler is starting to hit us and others when he is angry. We need advice and wonder what you have to say on this topic.

~Wondering: To spank or not to spank?

Dear Wondering:

Where to begin? How about: Nobody's perfect! I am a child of the 60s and 70s and recall that spanking, swatting and slapping were acceptable ways of managing children's behavior in the home and at school. Thankfully we have evolved and have learned that physical punishment has a very

---

negative effect on children and results in anger, aggression, damaged relationships and lowered self-esteem.

I have very strong feelings on the topic of spanking and any child punishment that involves physical, emotional and/or psychological abuse against children. I have researched many textbooks and literature over the years on discipline and punishment and must admit that our society is gradually coming to recognize the negative effects of punishing children physically.

Parents who spank their children think of it as an effective way to discipline. From my experiences, research and training, I think they are wrong, and so does the Canadian and American Academy of Pediatrics. Also, within our Canadian Criminal Code, Section 4 criminalizes violence against children if it exceeds "what is reasonable under the circumstances." Child protective services regard "any corporal punishment which results in bruising as child abuse."

Please note: I am not talking here about physical child abuse in your case or any other spanking incidents parents have shared with me. I'm talking about the ordinary kind of spanking that most parents think of as normal and helpful: two or three hard swats on the rear or a quick slap with your open hand against the rear.

In the short-term, spanking a child usually does get the child to stop the particular behavior you didn't like, and has a temporary effect of reducing the chance that the child will repeat the behavior. The child may have stopped misbehaving, but after the spanking he is likely to be crying, which may be almost as distressing as the original misbehavior.

In the longer term, the effects are clearly negative. First, when you spank, the child observes you using physical force as a method of solving problems or getting people to do what you want. You are your child's first teacher. Secondly, by repeatedly "pairing your presence with the unpleasant or painful event of spanking, you are undermining your own positive value for your child."

Spanking frequently carries a strong underlying emotional message—anger, rejection, irritation, and dislike of the child. Even very young children read this message very clearly. "Spanking helps to create a family climate of rejection instead of warmth, kindness and caring, with many negative consequences" (Helen Bee, *The Developing Child*).

I recommend the pamphlet, "What's Wrong with Spanking?" presented by the Department of Justice Canada and Public Health. It is free to parents and caregivers at your local health center, StrongStart center or Communities for Kids facilitator.

Please remember that you, the parent, are always learning. All parents need ideas and support, this parent included! Please remember that nobody's perfect!

~ *Ms. Barber*

Children need parents who say what they mean, mean what they say, and do what they say they are going to do.
~ Barbara Coloroso

Chapter Eleven

Parents: A Child's First Teacher

My grandmother once told me that being a parent will be the most rewarding job I will ever have, and it will be one of the most challenging. My grandfather also had wonderful quotes he would share generously and one of his favorites was that it's okay to make mistakes, just don't make the same mistake twice.

I wish that they had lived long enough for me to share my son with them, as well as the ups and downs, smiles and frowns I have experienced as a parent and the enjoyment and rewards I have received parenting my son. I have since discovered that they were both right, parenting is a joy and one of life's greatest rewards and challenges.

As a parent, we are our child's first teacher, helping them grow up to feel a sense of belonging and connection to their family and community while teaching them social and life skills they will need when they venture out to interact with others. I have always thought, felt and practiced a philosophy that became my vision as an early childhood educator, in that all children should and will learn, grow and develop to realize their full potential. I especially believe and govern my interactions and communications with children of all ages with this vision and philosophy and have raised my son in this manner.

Parenting our children is a full time, and occasionally frightening job. When our children are born, we are the first people that they interact with. We provide stimulating environments, experiences, and safe challenges that encourage a child's continuous development. Parents are mentors, guides, teachers, cheerleaders, coaches, tutors, and provide a safe and nonjudgmental environment where children can feel free to make mistakes. Children realize that, in the safety of a home with supportive, loving parents, they will not be judged and can therefore take on safe challenges and achieve many goals and develop many skills.

Education is defined as any experience which provides learning and growth to be achieved. Parents should view themselves as their child's first and most important teacher.

I have found that many simple everyday occurrences provide excellent opportunities to enhance your child's development. Remember, you are your child's first teacher, and never under estimate the value of even twenty minutes of quality time spent with your child.

Talk with your child about everything around you and respond with sentences using any words the child contributes from their vocabulary. Play games with the alphabet to introduce new letters. Tell stories about your childhood, or your child's favorite book, or a character within that story. When reading a story, describe what you see happening in the illustrations and storyline and ask your child what he thinks will happen next.

Let your child see that reading is fun and very enjoyable and extremely important to you. Read to them as long as the child's attention lasts. Be ready to read the same storybook over and over and over again. Discuss the front of the book, explain the role of an author, and talk about the illustrator's job in preparing the book. Point to the words as you read them and play games with the sounds. This is very important to your child's literacy and cognitive (intellectual) development.

(I will share more of my literacy and child development research and philosophies in my second book, *Dear Ms. Barber: Volume Two,* due out in

2016. I am also including research on attachment in this chapter, as well as a column about struggling with dressing a preschooler.)

The best way to start preparing a child for life and interactions outside of the home is by building a healthy, secure attachment bond with your child.

Attachment theorists Mary Ainsworth and John Bowlby define secure attachment as "an enduring affective bond characterized by a tendency to seek and maintain proximity to a specific person, particularly when under stress."

Current research in the area of attachment theory uncovered the fact that this unique relationship, the attachment bond, is a key factor in developing your infant's social, emotional, intellectual and physical well-being and should continue long after your child has grown.

As an adoptive parent, I also want to add that secure attachment can happen at any age and stage of childhood and this is true of my relationship with my son and myself as he was two and a half years of age when we first met.

Here's a fun column about helping a child learn age-appropriate skills.

Dear Ms. Barber:

We are struggling with dressing and getting our soon to be five-year-old ready with clothing in the morning before preschool and are worried that he is going to kindergarten in September and will not be able to get ready on time. We would love any advice or support you may have on this subject! Is it too soon to expect a four-year-old to put on his own pants properly, zip his own zippers and put on his own shoes on the proper feet, and how do we teach these skills?

~ Struggling with dressing a Preschooler

Dear Struggling with Dressing;

You are not alone in your struggle! I ask parents of preschoolers if they like to wrestle! If you spend any time getting a child dressed, that's probably what you are doing. Trying to get a small child to stand or sit still long enough so you can pull up pants or throw a shirt over their head can be, well, very trying.

The good news is, learning to get dressed is a sequence of lessons that most preschoolers master by the time they turn five. And like everything else, learning to get dressed is just another sequence of skills that young children practice and develop over time.

Not only do children have to develop certain gross and fine motor skills to master the technique of putting legs into pant holes or pulling up a zipper, they also need to start matching colors and recognizing how to choose clothing that will keep them warm or cool enough, all contributing to a growing sense of independence.

Learning to get dressed isn't a single skill that your child will learn overnight. Rather, it's a series of lessons that your child will grow to understand as they grow and mature.

Here are some approximate ages of when children figure out certain aspects of dressing themselves:

- starting to get undressed: 12 to 18 months old

- getting completely undressed without help: 18 to 24 months old

- pulling up pants that have an elastic waistband: 2 to 2½ years old

- putting on socks or a shirt: 2½ to 3 years old

- getting dressed and undressed with minimal assistance (including no-tie shoes): 3 to 4 years old

- dressing independently including any buttons, snaps, zippers or buckles: 4 to 5 years old

- tying shoes: between 5 and 7 years old

Don't stress if your child hasn't hit one of these milestones. These ages are simply guidelines and depend a lot on your child's gross motor skills, maturity and interest in the process.

Show and Tell

You may think because your child has been part of the process of you getting him dressed every morning that you can hand him a pair of pants and he'll pull them right on. And for some children, that may be the case. But for many children, a simple lesson in how the clothing should be used will do wonders.

Keep it easy. Show on yourself and then help your child get dressed, giving a running commentary on what you are doing: "Your pants have three holes. One at the top that goes around your waist and one for each leg. Make sure the tag goes in the back."

Simple is Best

To make the process simple, let your child learn on garments that are easy to put on. Loose-fitting clothes that don't have buttons, zippers or snaps are great to start off with. Elastic waistbands, large openings and pieces that have tags in the back (to avoid putting something on backwards) are also very little-child friendly.

Time and Patience Complete the Look

Make no mistake, getting dressed on your own is not an easy task. Even when a child has all the motor skills down, there is still a lot to think about. It's important to not rush them, especially in the days where they are just learning. Be patient and resist the urge to just get your child dressed yourself. The more you step in, the less they'll learn.

Mismatched Socks? Backwards Shirt? Praise, Praise, Praise

Learning to dress yourself is not a skill a child will learn overnight. And there can be some steps backwards. So if your child comes downstairs with her shoes on the wrong feet or pants that aren't buttoned, or are on backwards, help him fix what needs fixing, but also be sure to commend him for his great work and effort trying.

I recall a very funny moment early in my career as an early childhood educator with a preschool age boy in one of my preschool classrooms in my hometown. It was winter time and our cubby area was cluttered with snow boots, snow pants and jackets and this one boy had worked so hard at putting on his outdoor clothing all by himself. I gave him positive feedback on his effort and watched as his face beamed with satisfaction. I then glanced down at his winter boots and noticed that they were on the wrong feet.

Worried about how that might feel and the danger of him tripping outside on the ice and in the snow, I commented, "You have your boots on the wrong feet."

He glanced down at his feet and then back up to me and then down again at his feet. He had this puzzled look on his face and he said to me, "No I don't. These are my feet."

Well, it was everything I could do not to laugh as I quickly thought of how to help him understand left from right.

This young man is now in his early thirties and I had the extreme pleasure of seeing him again with his own young daughter in my StrongStart classroom along with his mother. We had a very good laugh when I shared this anecdote with him from all those years ago, and explained that I have shared this wonderful moment with many of my college students when we studied anecdotal recordings of children's behavior.

I need to remind all parents, caregivers and educators to document these wonderful moments when they occur for future reflections of amazing and memorable moments.

Enjoy every day and every moment on your journey through parenthood!

~ Ms. Barber

Parents are teachers, guides, protectors and providers for their children.
~ Iyanla Vanzant

Chapter Twelve

Shyness and Slow-to-Warm-Up Children

I have learned over the past thirty-five years in my rewarding field of early childhood education within my college classroom settings with my students, and within numerous early learning centers with young children that many psychologists and researchers have determined that there are three major types of temperament:

1. easy,

2. difficult, and

3. slow-to-warm-up.

Researchers have found that while all children show the same behaviors at some time, some children are more likely to show certain behaviors. They have found that about 60% of children fall into one of these three groups.

The easy child: These children show regular eating, sleeping, and elimination cycles, a positive approach response to new situations, and can accept frustration with little fuss. They adapt quickly to change, such as new food or a new school. They show a good mood most of the time, and smiled often.

Most of the problems reported with these children resulted when a child was placed in situations that required responses that were inconsistent with what they had learned at home.

The difficult child: These children show irregular eating, sleeping, and elimination cycles. They display a negative approach response to new situations, for example, frequent and loud crying or throwing tantrums when frustrated. They are slow to adapt to change, and need more time to get used to new food or people.

Most of the problems reported with these children center around socialization patterns, expectations of family, school, and peer groups.

If pushed to become immediately involved in a situation, these children are more likely to

exhibit loud refusal and sometimes opposi-
tional and aggressive behavior.

The slow-to-warm-up child: These children show negative responses of mild
intensity when exposed to new situations, but
slowly come to accept them with repeated exposure. They have fairly regular biological
routines.

Problems with these children vary depending
on the other characteristics they show. If
pushed to become immediately involved in a
situation, these children are more likely to exhibit withdrawal behavior of mild intensity,
such as clinging to the parent or hiding behind
them, quietly refusing to move, or retreating
to the corner of the room.

I have observed that children identified as shy or
"slow-to-warm-up" have the temperament characteristics of withdrawal, high sensitivity, and
low intensity. They are quiet and withdrawn in
social situations, offer fewer spontaneous comments, smile less, and interact less with peers.
Parents and teachers may perceive them as
anxious, frightened, or "shy." These children are
often overlooked. They do not cause disruptions,
are quiet and unassuming, yet they can need our
support just as much as active, intense and
aggressive "difficult" children.

I have also learned that about 40% of infants and children have an "easy" temperament and have observed that they readily approach and easily adapt to new situations, they react mildly to things, they are regular in their sleep/wake and eating routines, and they have a positive and happy overall mood. Easy infants make their parents feel as if they are doing a great job.

Approximately 10% of infants and children have the classification of "difficult" temperament, which again means that they withdraw from or are slow to adapt to new situations, they have intense reactions, they have irregular routines, and they have a more negative mood. They also tend to have long and frequent crying episodes. Parents of difficult infants may question their child care abilities and wonder what they are doing wrong.

The term "difficult" has a negative connotation as it overlooks what are often valuable behavioral traits: assertiveness, persistence and decisiveness. Other words I like to use are "spirited" or "feisty" and these terms have been suggested in my columns and within these chapters you are reading because they present as a more positive example; however, I use the word "difficult" here because it is the established term in the scientific research and literature I have studied and taught for many years.

Research states and my personal experiences have shown that between 5% and 10% of infants and children are in the slow-to-warm-up classification, in that they withdraw from or are slow to adapt to new things, they have a low level of activity, and they show a lot of negative mood when trying something new or meeting new people. I have observed that the slow-to-warm-up children do not like to be pushed into these new experiences and encounters and require time to adjust, settle in and feel comfortable. They are frequently thought of as shy or sensitive or somewhat withdrawn.

About 40% of children do not fit into any one category; instead, they have a combination of these qualities.

Parents and teachers are often concerned about children who are aggressive or present other negative and challenging behaviors in classroom settings. These are the "difficult" children and I have written a column on them and a chapter in *Dear Ms. Barber: Managing Children's Behavior, Volume Two.*

Withdrawing, sensitive or slow-to-warm-up children initially respond to beginning school or early learning/early childhood settings with hesitation and unease. In my experience, adjustment for these children can take anywhere from two weeks to two months or often more, depending on their level of withdrawal and sensitivity. The more often the sensitive child attends school or the early learning environment, the more quickly he becomes familiar, and familiarity with the setting, teachers, and children is the key to his feeling of getting settled. Illness or vacation, or a substitute teacher or caregiver, however, may start the process all over again.

These children are less likely to explore and experiment, though they are acutely aware of their surroundings and very observant. They try to avoid any reaction that they perceive as too loud, too frightening and too overwhelming.

Sensitive, withdrawing children prefer a quiet corner over exploring new territory because it limits their encounters with overwhelming stimuli social interactions with other children. Many prefer solitary play and they tend to keep to themselves, to stand back and watch rather than join in cooperative play. Often, the more uninhibited, outgoing children can dominate them socially.

Research shows that parents and caregivers who continually protect these children from minor stresses or who are overly concerned and anxious themselves, make it more difficult for the child to engage in social interactions or unfamiliar situations. A kind and firm approach without overreacting to their worry, uneasiness and lack of involvement while making age appropriate demands and understanding their temperament will greatly help "shy" or sensitive children become less fearful.

I recommend the following strategies and suggestions from my experiences with these children:

- **Avoid labels.** Saying "don't be so shy" is like saying, "Don't be yourself." As well, labeling your child in front of others as "shy" will reinforce this perception and can lead to low self-esteem as time goes on.

- **Look for opportunities to build your child's self-confidence.** Notice your child's interests, successes, skills, and milestones. Play together doing things your child enjoys.

- **Make time for your child to warm up to new caregivers.** Your child may never be the one who runs right into the babysitter's or childcare provider's arms when you are going out the door or entering the center. Plan ahead to help your child get better acquainted and comfortable with the caregiver.

- **Give notice about new people, events, and places.** Let your child know that her Uncle Bob is coming to visit, her friend's birthday is later that afternoon, or that she is moving to a new room for older children at child care next week. Letting your child know what to expect gives her a sense of control, which can reduce her anxiety.

- **Put what you think your child is feeling into words.** If a child seems reluctant to join another, you might say: "You are watching Jeff build his tall castle with blocks. Do you want to see if we can join in and help him?" If a child is standing away from your group activity you could say, "I like how you are watching our story at Circle Time. Would you like to come over and sit beside me so you can see the pictures?"

Here is a column I wrote on this subject. I hope my suggestions and experiences along with research and findings will help you to understand your slow-to-warm-up child better, and to support their development and journey through childhood.

Dear Ms. Barber:

Our three-and-a-half- year-old is painfully shy and we are worried that she will be shy and anxious her whole life and have trouble in kindergarten, if she does not learn how to make friends and socialize with other children.

She will be attending preschool in the fall and does not interact with other children. Do you have any advice or experiences to share that will help us support our child.

~ Very Concerned about Shyness

Dear Very Concerned:

I have worked with many shy and slow-to-warm-up children over the years and have found that some children take longer to adjust, and feel comfortable or safe with their new surroundings and friends.

We are all born with differences and this is true for personality and temperaments as well and shyness is a common occurrence with some children and adults.

"About 15 per cent of children are born with a nervous system that is like a tightly coiled spring," explains Dr. Robert Coplan, a psychology professor at Ottawa's Carleton University who researches shyness in pre-schoolers.

"They encounter something new and their heart rate ramps up and stays up. Even in non-stressful situations, their heart rates are a little higher than non-shy kids."

However, there are lots of things you can do to help your child feel more comfortable in social situations. Take small steps.

Start with a play date with one other child and have your child show the other something she knows how to do and is good at. Then, work your way up to larger groups.

Before she attends preschool or a regular lesson or activity, arrange for a one-on-one visit beforehand so she can experience the surrounding without additional stressors.

Most preschools and childcare centers also have a "staggered entry" or "gradual entry" where children attend with small groups at first for a short amount of time.

StrongStart centers and community centers offer programs where you can attend with your child and drop-in and leave when you need to and allow your child to explore social contact and interactions with other children and parents in a play-based environment.

Try to strike a balance between reassurance and independence. Shy children need time to feel safe and secure with new people and environments and it is advised to never push shy children to be "social butterflies" as this "pushing" them too soon can foster anxiety and added stress.

If you can, stay with your child for a while until she feels comfortable and then step back to the sidelines and reassure with smiles and positive body language.

I recommend the book *Nurturing the Shy Child*, by Barbara and Gregory Markway. They have developed a three-step process for developing and nurturing social skills in young shy children.

Step one is to identify social strengths and weaknesses. Step two involves practice and experiment with social skills with family members, and the third step suggests applying the social skills in real-life situations outside of the home and with others.

They also explain that while it's natural to want to explain your child's behavior by saying, "Oh, she's just shy," it's best to resist this temptation to label, because the child often sees it as an excuse not to try to be socially engaged. Instead you could say, "Anna is just taking a few minutes to check things out, but she'll be in there with the other children soon."

Shy children also pick up on the anxiety and stress from their parents and caregivers and this will add to their own fears and social anxieties.

Lastly, I also want to remind you that although we need basic social competencies to successfully navigate our world, your child can be naturally quiet and reserved and still function effectively with support and nurturance from caring adults and caregivers.

Enjoy your journey and seek support from others who have been on the same path.

~ *Ms. Barber*

In Conclusion

This book took almost two years to write. Many people encouraged me to choose my favorite columns and prepare chapters to complement the topics and to add any new ideas, research, stories and experiences so that I might be able to assist and support parents and caregivers during their journey through childhood.

I need to thank Yasmin John-Thorpe, a gifted author and dear friend I met in my hometown through the Raise A Reader program. She gave me sound advice and direction for my self-publishing adventure and introduced me to my competent and understanding editor, Norma Hill. Thank you Norma from the bottom of my warm heart for your positive feedback on my own grammatical skills and writing abilities and for sharing your wisdom and ideas in a very support-ive and encouraging manner. I apologize for the late night emails and the swift deadline for this first volume. We did it!

Some of you may also know that I love butter-flies. I had the pleasure of learning all about my favorite type, the monarch butterfly, first from a First Nations elder and secondly from visiting the Butterfly Wonderland in Arizona this past springtime with the love of my life. The monarch butterfly is the embodiment of spiritual growth and physical transformation perhaps more than any other life form on earth, because of the transformation from caterpillar to the beautiful version, butterfly.

You have probably noticed that they have been sprinkled throughout the pages of this book and one even landed on the shoulder of the little girl on the front cover. I have to extend a very special thank you to my typesetter, Dawn Renaud, for her passionate display of creativity. I am so pleased with the finished product of my first volume and Dawn treated this project as she would a young child. She nurtured, cared for and nourished a beautiful book. I will never forget the journey we shared.

I have already formally thanked my parents and son for their love and presence in my life and feel the need to thank my very special sweetheart, Kenny, for coming back into my life, at the most perfect time, and for loving me unconditionally. His never-ending love, support and friendship warms my heart daily.

He has been the positive driving force behind the completion of this book and encourages me every day with his thoughtful, caring, and often humorous manner.

I loved you yesterday,
I love you still,
I always have and
I always will.
~ Author Unknown

I love you, Kenny Thompson.

As I have mentioned throughout most chapters, my love and passion for children is strong, deep and true and comes from a place of understanding their needs and developmental stages along with a feeling of complete joy and amazement when I am with them.

As a parent, I too know how difficult it can be to be the best version of ourselves for our children and to want the best for them.

I truly believe that when we offer our children our time, our affection, our sense of optimism, and our unconditional love we help them find a way through any adversity along their journey.

I hope you have enjoyed these twelve chapters and columns as much as I thoroughly enjoyed preparing them for you.